This photograph. "Seven Barrows", a Bronze Age burial site, situated about three miles south of Highclere Castle, with Beacon Hill on the horizon.

Below. The remains of an Iron Age fort, on the north face of the summit of Beacon Hill, about one mile south of the Castle.

Highclere is an area which has been inhabited since prehistoric times and there is evidence of this both in Highclere Park and at Seven Barrows.

Seven Barrows, shown above, is the site of a Bronze Age burial ground. The remains of Bronze Age encampments have been found both to the south and north of Beacon Hill.

On the northern slopes of Beacon Hill are the remains of an Iron Age fort, complete with ramparts and ditches, looking downwards over what are now agricultural fields.

The first written records of the boundaries of the Estate were set out by an Anglo-Saxon King in 749AD. King Cuthred of Wessex granted an estate here to the Bishops of Winchester. They continued to own it for some 800 years.

Successive Bishops of Winchester built a substantial group of administrative buildings on the site of the current Castle and in the surrounding gardens, including a large medieval hall, a chapel and a series of domestic buildings and living quarters.

William of Wykeham

William of Wykeham, (1324-1404,) was one of the most outstanding figures in English history in the Middle Ages. He rebuilt much of the Manor of Highclere from 1368 in a grand style. He was one of the great Catholic prelates, who came from obscurity to become one of the richest and most powerful men in England.

Few contemporaries or later historians said anything against him. He was an architect, a builder, a man of business, a generous benefactor and a pious man. His character must have been uncommon, his morals recognised and his benevolence appreciated. He was Lord High Chancellor of England twice, responsible for the design and building of much of Windsor Castle and other Royal Palaces. He became the second richest man in England after John of Gaunt, Duke of Lancaster.

Indeed, he endowed New College Oxford (1379), because the Black Death had killed so many clergy and also Winchester College (1394). It is said that he used oaks felled at Highclere to build them.

Highclere was one of the Manors he "owned" whilst Bishop of Winchester. As the reign of Richard II staggered to its sad conclusion, the Pope appointed a new Archbishop of Canterbury, Roger Walden.

At Highclere, on February 1st 1398, William of Wykeham delivered the pall to the new Archbishop on behalf of Pope Boniface.

Right. Part of a 1611 map from the Archives in Highclere Castle showing the village of Highclere contained within the "Evinger Hundred".

An 'Hundred' was an area of the country from which the local noble could raise 'one hundred men-at-arms'.

The Herberts at Highclere.

After the Reformation, in the mid 16th century, Highclere passed from the clergy into secular hands and was owned successively by the FitzWilliam, Kingsmill and Lucy families. It was purchased in 1679 by Sir Robert Sawyer, Attorney General to Charles II and James II. He bequeathed the house and estate to his only daughter,

Margaret, in 1692, Her subsequent marriage to the 8th Earl of Pembroke brought Highclere into the Herbert family, ancestors of the Earls of Carnarvon.

Highclere Place House was at this time a double-fronted, Elizabethan brick mansion with a courtyard, stables, garden and orchards.

Margaret Pembroke's second son, Robert, inherited Highclere in 1706. Robert (pictured on page 23 as a child with his sister, Katherine) began to lay out a vast formal landscape including pleasure gardens and several follies. He was

succeeded by his nephew, Henry Herbert, who carried out many improvements to the landscaped park.

It is recorded that his cousin, the Earl of Pembroke and Montgomery, offered to send him "400 exotic tree seedlings called Cedars of Lebanon" in 1770. Henry replied "thank you for your nice offer but I pray you... send me 4,000 as I have plenty of room in my Park". He was sharply rebuked and told he was lucky to get any at all.

Above left. Sir Robert Sawyer, Attorney General to King Charles II.
Above centre, Sir Robert Kingsmill.
Above right, Lady Kingsmill.
Left. Andover Lodge, built in the 1740s by Robert Herbert, Sir Robert Sawyer's grandson.
Right. Sir Robert Sawyer's Parish Church.
Below. The layout of the Estate in the 18th century.

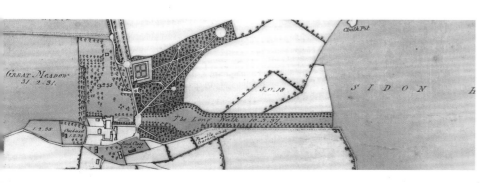

FROM GEORGIAN HOUSE TO VICTORIAN CASTLE

Major rebuilding works, carried out in the late 18th and early 19th centuries, converted the old brick and freestone house to a classical Georgian mansion within a pastoral setting. The major transformation, however, was just about to happen.

In 1838, the 3rd Earl of Carnarvon brought in Sir Charles Barry to transform his home into a grand mansion which would impress the world. It was a time of energy and change. The young Queen Victoria had just come to the Throne, and the whole decade witnessed innovation in political and cultural life. In architecture, new technology in the production of plate glass and wrought iron encouraged new forms of structural design.

By 1850, the re-modelled building (now called Highclere Castle) dominated its surroundings in a most dramatic way. No wonder Benjamin Disraeli's first words on seeing Highclere were "How scenical! How scenical!".

Henry Herbert, 3rd Earl of Carnarvon, painted posthumously, 1856.

Painted by James Edgell Collins (1820-1875), British Painter. He was a student of W.F. Wintherington and exhibited in London and Paris from 1841.

The 3rd Earl seated, with the newly completed mansion at Highclere rising proudly from the landscape behind him.

Barry did most of his work on Highclere between 1838 and 1843, but there were long delays at first, while Lord Carnarvon and he discussed and amended the plans for many aspects of the Castle's design.

In all, Barry prepared three different designs, the final one dated 1842 (the date carved over the front door: MDCCCXLII). It featured the great central tower which Barry had favoured from the beginning, but which Lord Carnarvon's land agent had warned was "pregnant with the most alarming danger to your Lordship's pocket".

Although the exterior of the north, east and south sides were completed by the time the 3rd Earl died in 1849 and Sir Charles Barry died in 1860, the interior and the whole of the west wing (designated as servant's quarters) were still far from complete.

The 4th Earl turned to the architect Thomas Allom, who had worked with Barry, to supervise completion of the interior and the west wing. Allom worked from some of Sir Charles Barry's original designs but also added ideas of his own and may have brought in other architects and designers.

He also built several new lodges in the Park, and a Memorial Chapel for the family, but plans to rebuild the Parish Church at the north-west corner of the Castle were abandoned.

The structural work on the interior of the Castle was finally completed in 1878. Once built, the Castle became a centre of political life during the late Victorian era. In the twentieth century, the Castle saw different uses during the two World Wars.

During the Great War, it was a hospital for wounded officers. During the Second World War, it was a home for evacuee children. The 6th Earl lived in the Castle until 1986.

The present (8th) Earl and Countess now live partly next door to the Castle and partly in the Castle, remaining closely involved in its day to day life and future.

Above. The Houses of Parliament in London, built by Sir Charles Barry.
Left. The front door to the Castle, featuring the date of build and the family motto: "Unc je Serviray", (Only One will I Serve).

Sir Charles Barry
(1795-1860)

He studied in London and abroad, mainly in Italy, and his work showed the influence of the Italian Renaissance. He was the pre-eminent architect of his time and his genius was recognised throughout Europe, for he was enrolled as a member of the academies in Rome, St. Petersburg, Berlin, Brussels and Stockholm.

He was knighted in 1852.

The Castle in 1857.

THE ENTRANCE HALL

Inside the great wooden doors, you enter a pure gothic entrance hall. The columns and vaulting make it quite unlike any other room in the Castle. It was believed to be designed in 1870 by George Gilbert Scott, who was also rebuilding the parish church at Highclere.

Scott was the architect of other buildings such as the Albert Memorial and St. Pancras Station in London. The polychrome floor was designed by William Butterfield, another well known Victorian architect and laid in March 1864 by William Field of London. The latter also installed an early but sophisticated central heating system.

The linked "C's" in the floor stand for the Latin phrase "Comes Carnarvon". The inter-twined "C's" are used by other Earldoms such as Cawdor and Cadogan.

A fine pair of terra-cotta wyverns (winged dragons with two legs and a scaly tail, the heraldic beasts of the Carnarvon family), flank the doors leading to the Saloon. More wyverns are carved on the ceiling amidst the heraldic shields (carved in 1861 by Mr Outhwaite of London) and also appear again and again throughout the Castle on carvings, firedogs and decorations.

Henry Herbert (later 2nd Earl of Carnarvon), c.1810. Painted by Thomas Kirkby, (1775-circa 1847).

Wearing the military dress of a Colonel of the West Somerset Yeomanry (a rank he held from 1803). MP for Cricklade, Deputy Lieutenant of Somerset, and High Steward of Newbury.

Elizabeth, 2nd Countess of Carnarvon, 1812. Painted by Thomas Phillips, (1770-1845).

Elizabeth Kitty, daughter and heiress of Sir John and Lady Harriet Acland, married the 2nd Earl of Carnarvon in 1796, thereby bringing the Somerset estates of Pixton and Tetton to the Herbert family.

Jeanie, 7th Countess of Carnarvon MBE, 2002. Painted by Valery Gridnev (b.1956).

She married the 7th Earl (then Lord Porchester) in 1956. Com-mitted to supporting both local and national charities, for which she was awarded the MBE in 2001, Lady Carnarvon founded the Newbury Spring Festival over 30 years ago. It is now one of the leading music festivals in Britain.

Henry, 7th Earl of Carnarvon, 2001. Painted by Valery Gridnev (b.1956).

Like his forbears, the 7th Earl developed a love of public service. He was tireless in his work at local level for Hampshire County Council, at regional level for the South East Regional Planning Authority and in the House of Lords, where he chaired several All-Party committees. He was the Queen's Racing Manager between 1969 and 2001.

A Marble Bust of the 2nd Earl of Carnarvon

The marble bust of the 2nd Earl of Carnarvon is by Lorenzo Bartolini (1777-1850). It was commissioned in Florence in 1819, while the family was on the "Grand Tour".

Lorenzo Bartolini emerged from humble beginnings to become the most highly esteemed Italian sculptor of the generation after Antonio Canova. Bartolini's great patron was Napoleon. After Napoleon's defeat and exile in 1815, he had few further commissions from France and Italy but, instead, undertook commissions from foreigners, often Russian or English.

Bartolini advocated "the Bello Naturale" school of creativity, inspired by nature, not bound by classical formulæ and constraints which reflected the Romantic poetry and literature of England at that time.

The double Library conveys an atmosphere of comfort, opulence and masculinity. It is no accident that the feel of the room is of a gentleman's club in London. Sir Charles Barry also designed the Reform Club library using the same dark mahogany-painted double column, gilded bookcases and rich red curtains.

Sir Charles Barry's detailed plans for this room were carried out after his death in 1860 by Thomas Allom, who had worked as Barry's co-architect on the Castle. During the construction of the Castle, it was used as the stonemason's workshop and it was also in this room that the masonry embellishments for the great Tower were prepared.

As today, local firms were employed where possible, from the marble fireplace to the interior decoration. For example, according to the building accounts for the "New Library", George Boyer of Newbury was paid a total of £632 2s 8d in 1875-6 for "polishing and gilding the bookcases in the large library, and supplying bosses and gilding for the ceiling".

The Castle was in its political heyday during the late Victorian period. At this time, the Library was used by the 4th Earl of Carnarvon as a "withdrawing" room. The Earl was an active Tory in parliament, a member of Disraeli's Cabinet in the 1860s, and Secretary of State for the Colonies in the 1860s and 1870s. Here, he could discuss politics with his friends and retire in peace.

Left. The elegant George III Carlton House desk (c.1780) sits in the Main Library. Such desks were said to have been designed in the 18th century for the Prince of Wales (who would later become George IV) by George Hepplewhite.

It is named after Carlton House, which was at the time the London residence of the Prince of Wales.

Above. The George III Rent table dates from about 1780. The 10 drawers around the table are divided alphabetically, in order to manage the rent collection from the estate tenants. They were very popular through the Regency and Victorian period.

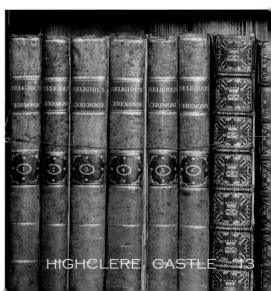

Henry, 1st Earl of Carnarvon, 1800.
Painted by Sir William Beechey
(1753-1839), English portrait
and landscape painter.

Sir John Acland as a young child, with pet
dog, c.1749. Painted by Thomas Hudson
(1701-1779), English Rococo-era painter.

Beechey trained to be a lawyer but turned to art and entered the Royal Academy schools in London in 1774.

In 1793, he became an associate of the Royal Academy and was further distinguished when he was made portrait-painter to Queen Charlotte and knighted 5 years later. His most spectacular painting was perhaps the review of the Cavalry by George III and his brothers, which was lost in the fire at Windsor Castle in 1992.

Colonel Henry Herbert had a talent for politics and was created Baron Porchester by George III after his calm handling of the Gordon Riots in 1780. Lord George Gordon, a Protestant political agitator, led a vast crowd in a march on Parliament during the first week of June 1780. The crowd wanted the government to repeal legislation permitting Catholic Emancipation.

Colonel Herbert was instrumental in defusing the hostility of the crowd and ensuring a peaceful outcome. In 1793,

Henry Herbert, Lord Porchester, was created 1st Earl of Carnarvon in recognition of his continued loyalty to the Crown.

This portrait (previously thought to be by Romney) is one of five family portraits by Sir William Beechey; the other four are in the Drawing Room.

Below. Part of the charter raised by King George III which granted the Earldom of Carnarvon to Henry Herbert.

Hudson studied under Jonathan Richardson, later marrying his daughter, much against her father's wishes! Hudson's students included Joshua Reynolds and among Hudson's friends were William Hogarth and Francis Hayman, who painted the Music Room ceiling.

To the surprise of many visitors this is actually the portrait of a young boy, who grew up to be a Major in the Grenadiers. He fought in the American War of Independence, was wounded and taken prisoner at the Battle of Saratoga in 1777. His wife, Lady Harriet, accompanied him throughout the campaign, stayed with him in captivity and returned with him to England in 1778.

Sir John died a few months later from the effects of a chill caught after a duel with a fellow officer, who had spoken disparagingly of his American captors. Sir John and Lady Harriet's daughter, Elizabeth, married Lord Porchester (later 2nd Earl of Carnarvon) in 1796. Elizabeth's portrait hangs in the Castle Entrance Hall.

During the Great War, when the Castle was turned into a military hospital for officers, the Library served both as a dayroom and dining room for convalescent officers.

During the Second World War, Highclere Castle housed evacuees from a school in Willesden, North London and, when air raids made it too dangerous for them to sleep on the top floor of the Castle, the younger children's cots were lined up in the Library. A teacher here at the time recalled the "wooden framework covered in hessian protecting the priceless books".

This room has also welcomed several Royal visitors over the years. In December 1895, according to the Sketch, the Library hosted "brilliant theatricals" in honour of the visit of the Prince of Wales (later King Edward VII 1902-1910). More recent visitors, as the family photographs show, have included HM the Queen and Prince Philip, Princess Margaret and the Prince of Wales. The present (8th) Earl of Carnarvon is HM the Queen's godson and, from 1969 to 1973, was her Page of Honour.

The Library contains about 5,650 volumes, many of them collected by the 4th Earl and reflecting his interests in history, politics, and travel.

One of the oldest volumes in the Library is the Italian writer Ariosto's Comedia: La Cessaria, dating from 1538. Many of the books on religious subjects belonged in to the 4th Earl's tutor and long-standing friend, John Kent, who had retired to Madeira but donated the contents of his own library (in thirteen large packing cases!) to Highclere in 1885.

Above. Several books written by the 4th Earl are bound in distinctive blue cloth and white vellum "Carnarvon" bindings.
Top left of page. The Library at Highclere Castle has hosted many famous guests. These extracts from the Visitors Book show Benjamin Disraeli, 1866, Charles Rolls, 1898 and Lt. General Cowans, Quartermaster General of the British Army, 1915.

THE MUSIC ROOM

The gold, silks and embroideries of the Music Room provide a strong contrast through the hidden door from the Library.

It is a wonderful south facing room with views towards two follies, Jackdaws Castle on the East Lawns and Heaven's Gate to the south on the summit of Siddown Hill which, at 943ft, is one of the highest points in Hampshire.

The walls are hung with Italian embroideries which were acquired from the Malatesta Palace in Rimini and are estimated to date from the 16th century.

The Malatesta family were prominent in Italy between 1295 and 1500.

The rooms is often used today for small lunch parties. It has been used in the past as a ping pong room and it was used by the 7th Earl to display the Egyptian Antiquities when the Castle first opened to the public in 1988.

Above. A detail from the embroideries in the Music Room.

Napoleon's desk

A unique piece of furniture in the Castle is the desk pictured below, which belonged to Napoleon Bonaparte.

Both the desk and chair were made by Jacob Frères of Paris, and perhaps came originally from Napoleon's rooms at the Palace of Fontainebleau.

This is an empire mahogany "fauteuil d'apparat" stamped "Jacob frères / rue Meslée" and was made between 1799 and 1803; the inscription reads "per Consul".

It is also stamped with "Palais des Tuileries" which specifically relates to the Empire period 1804 -14, because before and after

Napoleon in his study, anonymous drawing, Collection Lefeul, Paris

this 10 year period, it was called the "Chateau des Tuileries".

The Napoleon writing table of 1795, stamped G. Jacob, bears similarities to

other writing tables illustrated in sketches at this time. It has a plain leather top with ornate friezes of lion-inspired, simulated bronze supports either side.

Jacob Frères were famous French furniture makers run by Jacob-Desmalter and his brother, Georges Jacob II and produced many high quality pieces for the imperial residences of Napoleon and for many Royal Palaces in 18th century Europe.

The baroque ceiling was painted in the 1730's or 1740's. It must, therefore, have been commissioned by Robert Herbert for Highclere Placehouse, an Elizabethan house with a medieval hall and church, which he had inherited from his grandfather, Sir Robert Sawyer.

The rooms were likely to have been smaller, so, when it was removed and replaced in, firstly the Georgian and, later, the Victorian House, the Ceiling Paintings were cut and framed to extend them.

Francis Hayman

The ceiling was painted by Francis Hayman and depicts Athene Rising. Athene was the goddess of wisdom and arts.

Francis Hayman was an English painter and illustrator who became one of the founding members of the Royal Academy in 1768 and, later, its first Librarian.

He was able to paint different genres from portraits and landscapes, to scenes from history, literature and conversation pieces.

A contemporary of Hogarth, Hayman was born in Exeter, Devon. He began his artistic career as a scene painter in London's Drury Lane theatres, before establishing a studio in St. Martin's Lane.

A versatile artist influenced by the French Rococo Style, he achieved some note during the 1740s through decorative paintings executed for Vauxhall Pleasure Gardens in London.

This lovely south facing drawing room was very much the work of Almina, the 5th Countess of Carnarvon, in the late 1890's. She was the illegitimate daughter of Alfred de Rothschild and Marie Wombwell and it is no coincidence that this room bears a strong resemblance to some of the interiors at Halton, Alfred de Rothschild's Buckinghamshire house.

Alfred de Rothschild gave his daughter, Almina, a bolt of green French silk from which to cover the walls and make curtains. This had to be replaced in 1999, although it was matched as closely as possible to the original. The style is called "Rococo revival" and reflects a late Victorian fascination with the 'Ancien Régime' in France. The room is filled with family portraits, several of them by Beechey and important 17th and 18th century works by Kneller, Richardson and Reynolds.

Elizabeth, 1st Countess of Carnarvon, and her son, Algernon, 1796.
Painted by Henry Singleton (1766-1839). British Painter. Singleton was an artist in London. He achieved early success, exhibiting at the Royal Academy for the first time while still a student there and winning a gold medal for a painting while only 22 years old. Elizabeth Wyndham, daughter of the Earl of Egrement (of Petworth in Sussex) married the 1st Earl in 1771. Her youngest son, Algernon Herbert, was born in 1792.

Charles Herbert, c. 1789
Painted by Sir William Beechey (1753-1839). English portrait and landscape painter. Charles was the second son of the 1st Earl of Carnarvon and the boy in green in the group painting of the children on the page opposite. He was Groom of the Bedchamber to George III, and a lively member of Boodles Club in London. He joined the Royal Navy, was noted for bravery and received prize money for capturing pirates. He was accidentally drowned in 1808.

Children of the 1ˢᵗ Earl of Carnarvon, 1795

Right. Painted by Sir William Beechey (1753-1839). English portrait and landscape painter. He trained to be a lawyer but turned to art and entered the Royal Academy in London in 1774. In 1793, he became Portrait Painter to Queen Charlotte. The imposing 'Review of a Horse Guard with King George III and the Prince of Wales' (Royal Collections) earned him a knighthood in 1798, the year in which he was also elected a Royal Academician.

This group portrait is of the middle 4 of the 6 children of the 1ˢᵗ Earl and Countess of Carnarvon, with their pet dog Pincher, who looks as if he might have been rather a good guard dog. It hangs above the fireplace in the Drawing Room, opposite page. This painting has belonged to the Nation since 1988.

It is particularly interesting as it was painted as the children looked out of the window of the earlier Georgian house that predated the current Castle. Lady Frances Herbert was probably added at a later date.

The eldest son, Henry, Lord Porchester, is painted in the oval portrait in the Drawing Room and the youngest, Algernon, is in the portrait by Henry Singleton with his mother, opposite. Charles joined the Royal Navy, William became Dean of Manchester, and George became Rector of Highclere.

William, Duke of Gloucester, 1693

Left. Painted by Sir Godfrey Kneller (1646-1723). A leading portrait painter in England, he undertook portrait commissions from English monarchs from Charles II to George I, as well as other Royal patrons including Louis XIV and Peter the Great.

Born in Lübeck as Gottfried Kniller, he trained in Amsterdam, probably under Ferdinand Bol and in Rome. After arriving in London in 1676, he established himself as a baroque classicist portrait painter to Court Society.

William, Duke of Gloucester (1689-1700), was Queen Anne's sole child to survive infancy, although he only lived until he was 11. He was passionate about all things military, hence this portrait of him in a Roman tunic.

He commanded his own "army" of invited children, who drilled with wooden swords and marched to trumpets and drums at Kensington Palace.

The furniture is a mix of pieces from 1730-1900. The earliest pieces are the Italian bow-fronted walnut commodes and the English rams head centre table which are about 1730. The black lacquer cabinets are Chinese c. 1800, with later English stands. Lacquer furniture in the Chinese style was very fashionable in the late Victorian period.

An ebony cabinet is 18th century French with earlier painted panels showing personifications of two elements: land and water and the four continents: Europe, America, Africa and Asia. 18th century giltwood needlework chairs are English in the French style and so is the large brass and tortoiseshell inlaid cabinet, shown here at the top of this page, made in the style of Boulle, but dating from the 1870s.

Some of the paintings in this room are by William Beechey (1753-1839) who was, at the time, as famous as Gainsborough or Reynolds and enjoyed tremendous Royal patronage, especially during the 1790's. He exhibited at the Royal Academy in London every year for nearly 60 years, although he lived in Norwich with his 15 children.

Above. English Boulle-style cabinet, 1870, displaying 18th century Meissen china.

Right. "The Infant Bacchus", (Henry Herbert, later 2nd Earl of Carnarvon), 1775.

Painted by Sir Joshua Reynolds (1723-1792), English Rococo-era painter. Reynolds was one of the most important and influential of 18th century English painters, specialising in portraits and promoting the "Grand Style" in painting, which depended on idealisation of the imperfect. He was one of the founders and first President of the Royal Academy. George III knighted him in 1769.

Reynolds was born in Plympton St. Maurice, Devon, on 16 July 1723 and apprenticed in 1740 to the fashionable portrait painter, Thomas Hudson (whose portrait of Sir John Acland is in the North Library), with whom he remained until 1743.

Henry George Herbert (later 2nd Earl of Carnarvon), is depicted here as the infant Bacchus with two reclining lions by his side. The portrait was later engraved with leopards, and exhibited in 1844 as "Infant Bacchus with Tigers" but, when cleaned, revealed lions.

Page opposite. Robert Herbert (1697-1769), painted in childhood with his sister, Katherine, inherited the Estate from his grandfather, Sir Robert Sawyer (portrait on page 52). He embarked on a period of design and enhancement in the Park, focusing on using architecture and geometrical design to create observation points to "wonder at and admire" the landscape.

Katherine and Robert Herbert, children of the 8th Earl of Pembroke, by Jonathan Richardson, 1703.

Jonathan Richardson was a pupil of Kneller, and Richardson was in turn a teacher to Thomas Hudson (portrait in Library), Gainsborough and Reynolds. He was considered by his contemporaries to be one of the foremost masters of the day and retired a rich man, not only from his earnings as painter, but also from his earnings as a writer. He published the first significant work of artistic theory by an English author and, thus, is considered the key figure in the study of English Art Criticism. His approach to paint-ing these two children was to give them a "toy", in this case a dove, to amuse them during the sittings. This painting was restored to its former glory by the 7th Earl and Countess of Carnarvon in 1987. Another version of the portrait is on display at Wilton House, where the two children grew up.

Almina, 5ᵗʰ Countess of Carnarvon, the 'Florence Nightingale' of the Great War...

Almina Wombwell married the 5ᵗʰ Earl in 1895. She was extremely close to her father and very generous to others with her inheritance. She was an extraordinary lady, barely 5' tall, yet with boundless energy.

She had begun to devote herself to medical causes in about 1911 and was most interested in the work of eminent surgeons, such as Sir Bernard Moynihan. Just before the assassination of Archduke Ferdinand, on June 24th, 1914, Lord Kitchener had come to lunch at Highclere Castle.

In the event of war, Almina had decided that she wished to turn the Castle into a hospital. She wanted Kitchener to approve her plans. Her husband was not convinced, but Almina gained the financial backing of her father, Alfred de Rothschild.

She was able to purchase the latest equipment and pay for some 30 nurses under the direction of Dr Johnnie, their family doctor, supplemented by specialists from London.

Her patients adored her for the little touches, the whisky before supper, cleanliness, the kind (and pretty) nurses and for Almina's immediate efforts to contact their next of kin.

Above right. Alfred de Rothschild, father of Almina Wombwell, later the 5ᵗʰ Countess, shown on the opposite page.

A Captain David Campbell was billeted at Lady Carnarvon's hospital at Highclere, arriving with other wounded men after a painful two hour journey in a lorry from Southampton docks. He wrote in his diaries:

"The Countess of Carnarvon met us at the front door of her beautiful Castle and greeted us with kindest and most welcoming words ... we felt that we had come to a haven of rest, a veritable paradise ... she was an expert nurse having done two years training in a hospital ... what solace could be imagined for those so recently returned from the foul trenches of Flanders or the scorched hillsides of Gallipoli ... homemade beer was served at lunch and wine and whisky at dinner".

> YORK HOUSE, 24ᵗʰ June
> St JAMES'S.
>
> My dear Rothschild
> Very many thanks for your good wishes and also for the very charming birthday present which I shall always prize not only for its merits as a picture though they are great but more as coming from such a sincere & kind friend as you have been in these trying times – Always sincerely your
> Kitchener

Above. A letter to Rothschild from Field Marshall Lord Kitchener, Secretary of State for War, thanking Rothschild for his kind birthday present on 24ᵗʰ June.

Below left. A letter written by General Sir John Cowans G.C.B., G.C.M.G., Quartermaster-General of the Great War, to Alfred de Rothschild, father of Lady Carnarvon, 31st August 1915, praising Lady Carnarvon:

"Highclere Hospital - it is quite the best I have seen and its little Lady is a marvel, another Florence Nightingale..."

Here and on opposite page. Wounded officers from France, recuperating at Highclere Castle.

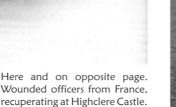

Once in the Smoking Room, you are again in the preserve of the Victorian gentleman.

It was usual from the late 18th century onwards for houses to have a separate room to contain the noxious fumes of tobacco and for gentlemen to gather for conversation and gaming. Ladies did not smoke.

Between the windows, a George II Rococo mirror hangs over an earlier French gilt wood table of about 1710. The large blue and gold vases on the mantlepiece are in the Chinese style so fashionable in the 1800s, but made in the Derby porcelain factory.

The model hare and partridge, in cold-painted bronze, were made in the Bergman factory in Austria in about 1900.

Right. This charming painted leather screen depicts nine different landscape scenes.

Throughout these scenes are fanciful menageries of farmyard animals in arcadian scenery, classical urns, sculpture and buildings, whilst characters from 18th century European characters stroll gently through the scenes.

There are three types of painting in the room:

The first is a collection of Dutch paintings from the 17th century, of which the most important is the large still life by Jan Weenix over the fireplace.

The second is a collection of 18th and early 19th century art brought back from the "Grand Tour", such as the views of Venice in the style of Canaletto.

The third is a series of paintings which show the Herbert family at Highclere and their cousins at Wilton House, dating from the Stuart period.

Above. There are three pictures in the manner of Bernardo Bellotto and Antonio Canaletto: Views of Venice (the Molo, the Doge's Palace (above) and the Piazza San Marco). These are typical mementoes collected on the Grand Tour, so popular in the early 19th century.

Charles I, Queen Henrietta Maria, William 3rd Earl of Pembroke and his brother Philip Herbert.

Painted by Richard Brompton (1734-1782), English Painter.

Other versions of this picture are at Wilton House and in the Royal Collection. The 3rd Earl of Pembroke was a staunch Royalist, and this grouping of the Herbert family with the King and Queen in Theobalds Palace, testifies to their influence in the early 17th century.

Philip Herbert, 4th Earl of Pembroke and his family.

[Painted by Sir Anthony Van Dyck (1599-1641), Flemish Baroque-era Painter].

A smaller copy of the great Van Dyck picture at Wilton. Given to the 1st Earl of Carnarvon by Ann Herbert, great grand-daughter of Lord Pembroke, in 1801.

The Italian marble 'pietre dure' table, inset with panels depicting birds and fruit, incorporates earlier (17th century) work, and its strong colour and pattern would have made it very appealing to the Victorians.

The top and front include a number of small panels of flowers and birds inlaid with semi-precious stones (pietre dure). This form of "painting in stone" was developed by the Florentines and the panels date from the 17th century.

Another charming description was "Pittura per l'eternità", painting for eternity. The panels were later set in a narrow border of jasper and then a further border of porphyry.

Porphyry is a stone quarried in Egypt for exclusive use of, initially, the Pharaohs and then of the Roman Emperors. The main quarry which provided this stone is located near to Qena, which is the area in which the ancient city of Thebes and the "Valley of the Kings" is to be found. It's name is derived from the Greek word for "purple".

Above. The Italian marble "pietre dure" table in the Smoking Room, with detail shown below.

Still Life Pictures by Dutch artist, Johannes Janson (1729-1784).

Hung above the Smoking Room fireplace, on either side of the 'Still Life' by Jan Weenix, are these old Dutch pictures of pastoral scenes.

Janson lived at Leiden in Holland and usually painted landscape and cattle, as here. Robert Herbert acquired these paintings for Highclere, presumably from the artist, as they are part of the original list of Works of Art as are most of the other Dutch paintings in this room.

Other furniture in the Smoking Room dates from the 1770s to the 1880s.

The corner cabinets are English, c.1780, incorporating panels of late 16th century German marquetry.

The table in the middle of the Smoking Room (shown below) holds occasional displays of Carnarvon family wedding photographs dating from that of the 6th Earl to the present Earl and Countess.

Still Life in a Park with dead swan, peacock and fruit, 1707.
Painted by Jan Weenix (1642-1719), Dutch Baroque-era Painter.

Jan Weenix was born in Amsterdam. His earlier work tended to be of harbour scenes in the manner of his father (also a well known painter), reflecting life in Amsterdam and Utrecht. Later on, Jan Weenix became known for meticulous still life paintings such as this scene, flooded with a warm, romantic light. He attracted noble patronage in both Holland and Germany. He often included architectural ruins and antique statues in his paintings, as here. Much of his work is in the Rijksmuseum, Amsterdam. The National Gallery in London owns three of his paintings, whilst another thirteen hang in the Wallace Collection.

George Villiers, 2nd Duke of Buckingham, and his brother Francis, when children. Painted by Sir Joshua Reynolds (1723-1792), English Rococo-era painter.

This painting is a homage to Van Dyck. Joshua Reynolds felt an affinity to the great Master. The Herbert family were great Van Dyck patrons during his lifetime.

These are the children of the 1st Duke of Buckingham who was a close friend of James I and Charles I, but was deeply unpopular.

The Duke was eventually assassinated in Portsmouth in 1628.

The two children were raised with the Royal Family in exile, in France, during Cromwell's Commonwealth.

THE MORNING ROOM

The 7th Countess redecorated this room in 1988-9 to create an intimate feminine sitting room, using shades of soft green and chintz to complement the 19th century plasterwork.

The colours for the walls were taken from the exquisite portrait, by Simon Elwes, of the 7th Earl's American mother, Catherine Wendell. The room has another American link through the 7th Countess of Carnarvon.

Jeanie, Lady Porchester, later 7th Countess of Carnarvon, 1964.
Drawn by Molly Bishop.

Jeanie, Countess of Carnarvon, MBE, married the 7th Earl (then Lord Porchester) in 1956. Living at Highclere, she returns each year to her Wyoming ranch in the USA, where she grew up, the daughter of the Hon. Oliver Wallop.

Her grandfather, the Earl of Portsmouth, raised horses in Big Horn, Wyoming and her brother, Malcolm Wallop, was until recent years, Senator for Wyoming.

Almina, 5th Countess of Carnarvon.

Catherine, 6th Countess of Carnarvon, 1929.
Painted by Simon Elwes (1902-1975).

Catherine Wendell married the 6th Earl of Carnarvon in 1922. Elwes was a fashionable portrait artist of the Twenties.

The Countess of Chesterfield with her daughter, the 4th Countess of Carnarvon, standing on a balcony.
Painted by J J Chalon, RA (1778-1854).

Chalon was Swiss-born but lived in England, studying at the Royal Academy with his brother, AE Chalon, who became "Portrait water colourist" to Queen Victoria.

Thus, both brothers were very well known and both exhibited in London for some 50 years.

The bureau to the right is probably one of the rarest pieces of furniture in the house. It was made of kingwood in 1765 by Pierre Langlois (1738-1781), famous French cabinet maker.

The fashion for inlaid and ormolu enriched furniture was accentuated by the French ébéniste, Langlois.

Based in Tottenham Court Road, London, from the 1750's, Langlois specialised in furniture which, according to his trade advertisement, 'enjolivee de ornement de bronze doree'.

Langlois became the most renowned Cabinet maker of his time, bringing quality and Parisian style to English furniture. His business flourished and he enjoyed enormous success.

Commissions enjoyed by Langlois included work supplied to the Royal Family, the Dukes of Northumberland and Bedford, the Earl of Coventry and the Marquis of Zetland.

Fiona, 8th Countess of Carnarvon.
Sketch by Paul Benney, 2005.
Born in 1959, Benney has lived and worked in New York as well as London. Established as one of the most successful portrait painters in the UK, he has exhibited in major galleries in London, New York and Barcelona as well as winning BP awards at the National Gallery three times and painting many well known people on both sides of the Atlantic.

THE RED STAIRCASE

Evelyn, 4th Countess of Carnarvon, painted posthumously in 1877.

The Hall houses portraits of members of the family and their friends. From it, the Red Staircase leads to the main bedroom floor above, and to the former nursery, schoolroom and additional bedrooms above that. The servants were expected to use the plain stone stairs on the other side of the house.

Left. Portrait painted by John Rogers Herbert (1810-1890). Herbert, who had studied at the RA Schools, began by painting portraits and romanticised subjects from Italian history. He was Master of the Government Schools of Design and was commissioned to paint frescoes for the new Houses of Parliament. Herbert exhibited over one hundred paintings at the RA between 1830 and 1889.

Right. Portrait painted by The Hon. Mr. Graves.
Lord Chesterfield was the brother of Evelyn, the 4th Countess of Carnarvon.

George, 7th Earl of Chesterfield, painted posthumously in 1872.

Lady Evelyn Stanhope married the 4th Earl of Carnarvon in 1861. Her brother, Lord Chesterfield, pictured opposite, died in 1871 and, sadly, she died just after the birth of her fourth child, Victoria, to whom Queen Victoria stood as Godmother.

Her eldest daughter was 10 years old, her son, in future to become the famous 5th Earl, the Egyptologist, was 9, her third child 4 years old and her baby daughter 3 weeks old. He husband was devastated and retired from politics to support his children.

Evelyn's mother was the Dowager Countess of Chesterfield and, upon her later death, she left the Chesterfield estates in Nottinghamshire to her grandson, who later became the 5th Earl of Carnarvon. It was much of this wealth which her grandson spent to finance the years of excavation in Egypt.

In 1878, the widowed 4th Earl married Elizabeth Howard as his second wife and had two sons, Mervyn and Aubrey Herbert. Aubrey was an extraordinary scholar and linguist and a fearless soldier during the Great War. He was MP for Yeovil and a great friend of the Asquiths and also of writers such as John Buchan. Buchan based his character and book "Greenmantle" on Aubrey.

In 1915, Aubrey returned to Highclere to be nursed from injuries in the Great War. He inherited the Pixton Estate on Exmoor. He died of septicaemia on 23rd September 1923, following a minor operation to remove a tooth.

Henry, 6th Earl of Carnarvon, 1941.
Painted by David Jagger (d.1958).

Wearing the uniform of the 7th Hussars. A great raconteur and convivial host, the 6th Earl lived here until his death in 1987.

Henry, Lord Porchester, later 7th Earl of Carnarvon, 1941.

Painted by David Jagger (d.1958).

Fiona, 8th Countess of Carnarvon, 2007.
Painted by Tin Odescalchi.

Tin (Christina) trained at the Gloucestershire College of Art, then the Akademie den Bildenden Kunst in Vienna, under Rudolph Hausner. She has exhibited in London, Edinburgh, Chicago and Hong Kong.

George, 8th Earl of Carnarvon, 2000. Painted by Valery Gridnev (b.1956). Russian Painter. After military service, he returned to Sverdlovsk and entered Art College. In 1982, he was accepted at the Repin Institute of Painting, Sculpture and Architecture in St. Petersburg. One of his graduation paintings, 'Early Years', won him a prestigious prize - the Gold medal of the Academy of Arts in 1990.

THE GALLERY & GALLERY BEDROOMS

The Gallery at Highclere Castle with its 50' high vaulted roof overlooking the Saloon.

re-decorating the Gallery and bedrooms to recreate the standard of furnishing that any guest visiting Highclere would have enjoyed in the past, using original fabrics and retaining the detail from previous generations.

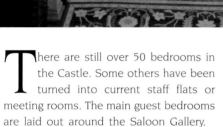

There are still over 50 bedrooms in the Castle. Some others have been turned into current staff flats or meeting rooms. The main guest bedrooms are laid out around the Saloon Gallery.

Some of the bedrooms are named to commemorate visits from the members of the Royal Family, others are named for ancient Anglo-Saxon Kingdoms. The 8th Countess of Carnarvon has been steadily

Jean de Boisgelin,
Archbishop of Aix la Chapelle
(1752-1804).

Painted by Henry Howard.

The parents of the 1st Earl of Carnarvon were married in Aix and, presumably, de Boisgelin became a family friend. He took refuge at Highclere during the French Revolution.

He returned to France in 1801 and became a Cardinal in 1803, just before he died. He was a literary man and an excellent Church administrator known for his wisdom and generosity.

Opposite and below. Details from the Gallery Belgian tapestries and corridors.

Mercia

Mercia is one of a group of 4 linked rooms running along the south side of the house.

Arundel

The Arundel bedroom was used as an Operating Theatre during the Great War.

The Herbert bedroom once formed the 4th Earl's Upper Library, linked to the main Library below by a spiral staircase.

Herbert

The opulent Stanhope bedroom is decorated in rich red, recalling its decoration for the visit of the Prince of Wales in December 1895.

Stanhope

THE OAK STAIRCASE

Mrs. Musters by Reynolds.

The Oak Staircase is dominated by Sir Joshua Reynolds' portrait of Mrs. Musters, a famous 18th century actress, as Hebe, the Greek goddess of youth.

Sir Joshua Reynolds painted the famously beautiful Mrs. Musters several times. She is portrayed in the guise of Hebe in a rather dramatic and windswept setting and pose.

Henry, 2nd Earl of Carnarvon

Painted by James Edgell Collins.
The 2nd Earl (1772-1833) was a keen traveller and politician. He married the heiress Elizabeth Kitty Acland (whose portrait hangs in the Entrance Hall of the Castle, see page 10). He was active in the House of Commons, before succeeding to the Earldom and was active in the House of Lords thereafter.

He was a Whig for most of his life but, protesting against parliamentary reform (1831 Bill), he became a Tory.

The Oak Staircase is situated at the base of Sir Charles Barry's Great Tower.

Thomas Allom's great Oak Staircase fills the tall Italianate Tower that Sir Charles Barry built, to look as if it was at the centre of the new house (it is actually slightly to one side), in 1842.

Messrs. Cox & Son of London took nearly a year to carve and install the staircase, between December 1861 and October 1862.

Late 17th century Brussels tapestry depicting the story of Meleager.

Above the Oak Staircase hang two of the 17th century Brussels tapestries (continued in the Saloon) depicting a Greek Myth, the story of Meleager. The Brussels workshops were renowned for producing complex and beautiful tapestry designs from the early years of the 16th century.

Greek myths provided excellent subject matter, with visualisations of dramatic scenes and lifesize figures acting out moments of immense physical and emotional drama in a realistic landscape woven with accurate perspectives. The story of Meleager is told in the two large tapestries and four smaller ones, hung high around the Saloon, which continue the story.

According to Ovid, Oeneus, King of Calydon, offended the goddess Diana, by sacrificing to Bacchus rather than to her. In revenge, she sent a large boar to ravage the Kingdom, until it was slain by Meleager, his uncles and the huntress Atalanta. Since she had fired the first arrow to wound the boar, Meleager awarded the boar's head to Atalanta. His uncles, however, thought the trophy should be theirs and seized it from her, whereupon Meleager, in anger, killed them. This tapestry and its companion on the opposite wall, show Oeneus sacrificing to Bacchus and Meleager's mother burning the log of life (thereby assuring Meleager's death), after he had slain her brothers in the dispute over the boar's head.

The four smaller tapestries around the Saloon Gallery continue the myth of Meleager: two depict the boar hunt, one depicts Atalanta's attendant adjusting her sandal and the fourth depicts Meleagers's sisters mourning his death.

Italian marble statue of Henry, later 4th Earl of Carnarvon and his sister Eveline, sculpted by Tenerani, 1838.

On the lower flight of the Staircase is a marble statue of the 4th Earl of Carnarvon as a child, and his sister Eveline, commissioned from the Italian sculptor, Pietro Tenerani (1789-1869), who studied under Bartolini, (see page 11), while they were on a visit to Rome with their father in 1838. Eveline later married the Earl of Portsmouth and her great grand-daughter, Jean Wallop, married the 4th Earl's great grandson and became the 7th Countess of Carnarvon, thereby linking the two families again.

The Saloon in Highclere Castle is the heart of the house. It was designed for the 4th Earl by Thomas Allom in a gothic style, with rich decoration and was completed in the 1860s.

It may well have been inspired by the Medieval hall which stood here and formed part of the interior of the Georgian house. The gothic architecture incorporates the coat of arms of the Carnarvon family.

The painted heraldic shields around the Gallery depict the coats of arms of the Herberts, beginning with the 1st Earl of Pembroke who married Anne Parr, (Katherine Parr's sister and, therefore, sister in law to Henry VIII) and progress towards those of the present Earl and Countess of Carnarvon.

Left. The Saloon gallery is lined with the heraldic shields of the Herbert family. This 'Three Doves' shield shows the coat of arms of Margaret Sawyer and the 8th Earl of Pembroke. Margaret Sawyer's portrait is described on page 52.

Right. This heraldic shield, featuring the 'Three Boars' emblem, shows the coat of arms of the 1st Earl of Pembroke and Anne Parr. There are 20 shields in total.

Henry, 4th Earl of Carnarvon, c. 1880s.

Painted by Frank Holl (1845-1888),
British Social Realist Painter.

Born in London, Holl was a mainstay of the Graphic, a weekly illustrated newspaper in the 1870s. The 4th Earl is shown here in a Peer's Robes and holding a quill pen.

The 4th Earl of Carnarvon served in all the Conservative governments between 1858 and 1886. An outstanding classicist, he undertook translations of the Agammenon and the Odyssey. The Library here at Highclere reflects his catholic tastes: there are books he collected by Italian, French and English authors.

Lord Carnarvon knew many of the literary figures of the time, including Robert Browning, Charles Kingsley, Walter Bagehot, Lord Tennyson and George Eliot. Henry James came to Highclere to visit Lord Carnarvon's widow just after his death.

His obituary in "The Times" commented he was "born to fill a prominent place in a complex society and to keep in touch with many and diverse interests … It could be said of him that he was too conscientious for partisanship and too scrupulous for political success".

Evelyn, 4th Countess of Carnarvon, 1875.
(1834-1875). Portrait by Henry Graves.
Seated against a landscape and reading a book.
The portrait was painted the year the Countess died.
They had four children: Lady Winifred, George, later the 5th Earl, Lady Margaret and Lady Victoria.

Elizabeth, 4th Countess of Carnarvon.
(1856-1929)
After the premature death of his first wife in 1875 at the age of 41, the 4th Earl of Carnarvon married Elizabeth Catherine Howard in 1878. They had two sons: Aubrey and Mervyn.

Henry, 3rd Earl of Carnarvon, painted posthumously in 1856. Painted by James Edgell Collins (1820-1875). He was a student of W.F. Wintherington and he exhibited in London and in Paris from 1841.

Barry's architectural plans are visible at the Earl's elbow, and Highclere Castle can be seen in the background. The 3rd Earl was a great adventurer and a linguist, travelling throughout his life in Europe, Turkey and North Africa. He was fascinated by Moorish architecture, and wrote a tragic play and several poems about Spain and the Moors.

Henrietta Anna, 3rd Countess of Carnarvon (1804-1876). Eldest daughter of Lord Henry Thomas Howard-Molyneux-Howard, Deputy Earl Marshall to King George III and King George IV, she married Lord Porchester (later to become the 3rd Earl) in 1830.

Gilt leather must be one of the most splendid and now one of the rarest wall hangings. Such panels were made between the 16th and 18th centuries. Firstly, the leather was entirely covered with a very thin layer of silver leaf; then

it was covered with a yellow varnish, thus creating a 'golden surface'. Afterwards, a pattern was printed on the surface and painted with different colours. From 1628 onwards, a metal mould was used and embossed gilt leather, as at Highclere, was the result. Since the leather is in squares rather than glued together to form strips, it suggests the wall-hangings were made before 1680.

The art of making wall hangings originated in Cordoba in Spain, where a uniquely soft leather gave the artists versatility. Whilst some panels are still preserved in various museums, the complete decoration of the Saloon in Highclere Castle is exceptional.

Right. A close-up of the ornate embossed and gilt leather.
Left. A detail from the Spanish leather and gilt wall coverings.

Below. The stone fireplace and corbels were carved by Mr Outhwaite of London, who also carved the heraldic ceiling in the Entrance Hall. Right. One of two matching cabinets in the Saloon. Above. A detail from a bronze and gilt table lamp.

THE DINING ROOM

This room was transformed by Sir Charles Barry into the "Stuart revival" style of interior decoration.

The room was redecorated by Jeanie, the 7th Countess of Carnarvon, bringing warm yellow silks to the north facing room, highlighting its grandeur and opulence.

The room is dominated by Van Dyck's great equestrian portrait of Charles I. Also on display in the room, are portraits of some of Herbert ancestors who lived and took part in the English Civil War (1643-1647) and then managed to remain courtiers and politicians under the reign of Charles II, 22 years later.

Much of the furniture was built for the room and the centrepiece is the dining table of c.1870, which contains a mechanism to include twelve extending leaves.

18th century pieces include the long case clock by Shelton, serving table and mahogany side chairs.

John Shelton made five longcase clocks for the Royal Society to use for timing the transits of Venus in 1761 and 1769 from different parts of the world. These clocks travelled extensively and were used in various experiments to determine the shape and mass of the Earth.

Captain Cook took one of the clocks on his first voyage and two on each of his other two voyages.

Left. The longcase clock in the State Dining Room, made by John Shelton, London.

The English Civil War (1643-1647) was a frightening period in which to live. Families were often split with close relatives fighting on different sides.

Robert Dormer, the 1st Earl of Carnarvon, was a Royalist Cavalier, which is clearly shown in his portrait, flowing hair and flamboyant clothes. He was killed fighting for Charles I. His father in law, the 3rd Earl of Pembroke, whose portrait hangs the other side adjacent to Charles I, was also a staunch Royalist.

His brother in law, however, whose portrait hangs above Margaret Sawyer, was a senior parliamentarian and one of the two men sent by Cromwell to persuade Charles I to surrender on 2nd January 1647.

Another Herbert relation, Thomas Herbert, was appointed by the Parliamentarians to act as courtier/guard to Charles I, sleeping in his room during the last 18 months of the King's life.

King Charles I on horseback, accompanied by Chevalier le Sieur de St. Antoine.

Painted by Sir Anthony Van Dyck (1599-1641), Flemish Baroque-era Painter.

There are several other versions of this painting. One is in the Royal Collection, a second is at Warwick Castle and another at Montecute House. In the Dining Room, to the right of Charles I's portrait, is William Herbert, 3rd Earl of Pembroke who was, unlike his son, a great Royalist.

The Princesses Elizabeth and Anne, youngest children of Charles I.

After Sir Anthony Van Dyck.

Princess Elizabeth was just 13 when her father was executed and she had been held in Parliamentarian hands throughout his imprisonment, whilst her mother was in France with her elder siblings. This is a copy of part of the picture in the Royal Collection.

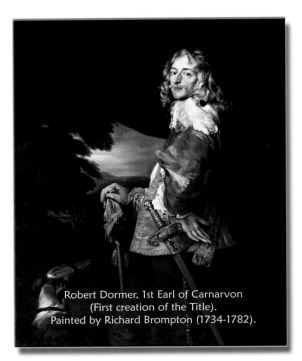

Robert Dormer, 1st Earl of Carnarvon
(First creation of the Title).
Painted by Richard Brompton (1734-1782).

Anna Sophia Herbert, daughter of the 4th Earl of
Pembroke, married the 1st Earl of Carnarvon.
Painted by Sir Anthony Van Dyck (1599-1641).

He fought on the King's side in the Battle of Newbury in 1643, was mortally wounded and died at the Bear Inn in Speenhamland, the King at his side. The Earldom became extinct on the death of his son in 1709. It was revived by James Brydges in 1714, but became extinct in 1789. A new line of Earls of Carnarvon was established with Henry Herbert in 1793, whose portrait is shown on page 53.

Although they never owned or came to Highclere, there is a link between the Dormer and Herbert Earls of Carnarvon. Anna Sophia, who married Robert Dormer in 1625, was the daughter of Philip Herbert, 4th Earl of Pembroke. There is a full length portrait of her by Van Dyck at Chatsworth.

Sir Robert Sawyer.
His hand resting on the head of his greyhound.
Painted by John Riley (1646-1691).
English Baroque-era Painter.

Margaret Sawyer, 8th Countess of Pembroke. c. 1685
Painted by Sir Godfrey Kneller (1646-1723),
German-born, English Baroque-era Painter.

Sir Robert was MP for Wilton and Attorney-General to Charles II and James II. He purchased Highclere from the Lucy family in 1679, rebuilt the ruined Parish Church, laid out the grounds and in 1692 bequeathed it to his daughter, Margaret Sawyer. He bought the Highclere Estate to be close to Charles II, when the King moved his Court from London to Winchester.

He served all the rulers from Charles II to George I while also portraying Louis XIV and Peter the Great. Born in Lübeck as Gottfried Kniller, he trained in Amsterdam and in Rome. She was the only daughter of Sir Robert Sawyer and died in 1706, leaving Highclere to her second son, Robert Sawyer Herbert. There is an old family legend that, if this portrait is ever moved, disaster will strike the Herberts.

Henry Herbert, 1st Earl of Carnarvon.
(third creation).
[Painted by Thomas Gainsborough (1727-1788).
English Rococo-era / Romantic Painter.

Gainsborough was a painter of portraits, landscapes and fancy pictures, one of the most individual geniuses in British art.

Portrait completed by Gilbert Stuart (1755-1828), American Painter. Stuart was famous as the painter of the portrait of George Washington which is to be found on US dollar bills.

Like all the Herberts, Lord Carnarvon had a talent for politics and had been created Baron Porchester by George III, after his calm handling of the Gordon Riots in 1780.

In 1793, he was created 1st Earl of Carnarvon in recognition of his continued loyalty to the Crown.

The ornately carved chimneypiece has barley twist columns made from two logs of coromandel wood, presented to the 2nd Earl in 1822 by Mr. Saram of Colombo, Ceylon who had known Lord Carnarvon as a student.

The 4th Earl later noted that he had apparently intended to offer a gift of an elephant, but was persuaded against it!

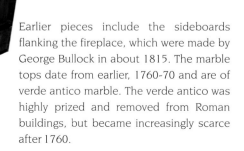

Earlier pieces include the sideboards flanking the fireplace, which were made by George Bullock in about 1815. The marble tops date from earlier, 1760-70 and are of verde antico marble. The verde antico was highly prized and removed from Roman buildings, but became increasingly scarce after 1760.

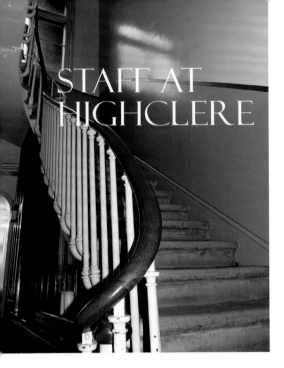

STAFF AT HIGHCLERE

A little over 100 years ago, Highclere Castle was part of the centre of the English world during Victorian and Edwardian times and the British Empire was at its zenith.

The staff at Highclere were looking after guests from Royalty to politicians, Prime ministers, writers, Egyptologists, aristocrats, scientists, aviators and adventurers. It had to be a very well run operation. Guests arrived with their valets and chauffeurs, lady's maids and grooms; all had to be catered for.

The top floors of the Castle has some 50-80 bedrooms. Perhaps thirty-five were used by the Carnarvon family and their guests. The remainder were used by the staff. The maids lived on the top floors and the footmen in the back wing. Married staff moved out to cottages in the Park.

The Estate was managed by Lord Carnarvon's agent, Major James Augustine Rutherford, who looked after all the aspects from the farming to the forestry, property, the Castle, the Stud and associated costs and revenues.

Leaving the Saloon, near the Dining Room there is another stone staircase behind a Green Baize door. The stone staircase was used by the staff. It winds up some 3 floors and downstairs to what used to be the Staff Dining room, scullery and the "below stairs" area of operations.

Within the Castle, the Butler, Lord Carnarvon's Valet and the Housekeeper reigned supreme. The Butler (known at Highclere as the House Steward) from the time of the 5th Earl of Carnarvon's marriage in 1895 until the Earl's death in 1923 was Albert Streatfield. The precedence of the

Earl and Countess determined the precedence of the staff at the staff dining table (below): the House Steward, Mr. Streatfield, and the Housekeeper, Emma Bridgeland, sitting in the centre facing each other, Lady Carnarvon's maid to the right of Streatfield, Lord Carnarvon's valet to the right of the Housekeeper).

Initially, Streatfield lived in the Castle, but when he married Edith Andrew in 1897, he moved into a cottage in the Park. Nevertheless, he retained his sitting room in the Castle (now part of the Tearooms). Streatfield was responsible for the smooth

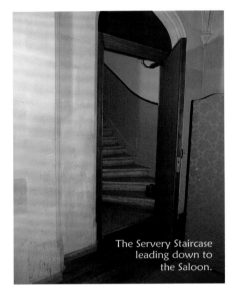

The Servery Staircase leading down to the Saloon.

running of the Castle. Also, he was in charge of waiting on Lord Carnarvon and family at dinner and of looking after the wine cellar.

He was expected to announce visitors, take calling-cards, escort visitors out of the House, organise the post and to supervise the closing of the Castle each night, ensuring that all doors, windows and shutters were locked, closed and bolted.

The staff dining room in the cellars of the Castle.

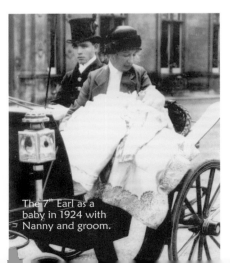

The 7th Earl as a baby in 1924 with Nanny and groom.

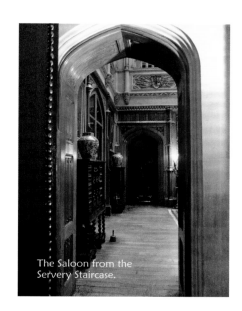
The Saloon from the Servery Staircase.

Castle staff on an outing to Beacon Hill Gate, c. 1900.

including them where they shouldn't be … He was the typical, efficient English butler of that period".

Fernside began as a footman in the Castle and, in 1893, became the 5th Earl's valet. Later, in 1923, he succeeded Streatfield as Butler. Completely loyal and discreet, Fernside handled all Lord Carnarvon's personal affairs and managed his personal

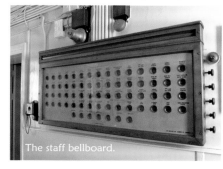
The staff bellboard.

The 6th Earl grew up in Streatfield's time and describes him as "gravely deferential and prepared at all times to deal with all exigencies." He had mutton chop whiskers, and was described as "pedantic and dropping "h's" where they should be and

accounts. He looked after Lord Carnarvon's wardrobe, packed and organised his travel arrangements and travelled with him.

Highclere Castle footmen wore smart navy liveries with Carnarvon crested buttons. Immaculately presented at all times, with clean clothes, clean-shaven faces and smartly brushed hair, they answered directly to Streatfield.

They assisted Streatfield with the arrival and departure of visitors, served the family at dinner, helped at parties and cleaned the silver, glass and chinaware.

The Staff of Highclere Castle, c. 1896.

The Outside Staff at Highclere Castle: Gamekeepers, Foresters, Gardeners...

During the period before the Great War, the wages books record the employees according to the different departments.

There were 19 Gamekeepers under Henry Maber, Head Gamekeeper, who passed the role to his son and grandson.

There were 20 Gardeners under the Head Gardener, William Pope, who won many local prizes (picture on opposite page). Samuel Ward (1840-1937), senior Gardener, lived in a Cottage in Highclere Street and his son was possibly the Hall Boy in the Castle.

Another local family, the Digweeds, were gardeners at Highclere over several generations. The name G. Digweed appears on the Estate Roll of Honour for the Great War.

Thirty men worked in the Forester's department under the Head Forester, William Storie. The saw mill was re-equipped and, as with the gardeners, many local families worked on the Estate over several generations.

Coachman Henry Brickell had an under-coachman, Woodley, and 4 or 5 grooms and a stable boy. Most of them lived above the Stables in the courtyard.

Left. Highclere Gamekeepers, Henry Maber (left), with his brother John. Henry became head gamekeeper on the Highclere Estate in 1896. He died in 1923 and passed on his role to his son Charles, pictured top right with the 6th Earl.

Below left. An page from Henry Maber's ledger book from 1911/12: first entry, "Pair Scotch Knickers... £1, 1s, 0d"!
Below right. Highclere Estate workers standing by the Garage in Edwardian times.

Above. Highclere Gamekeeper, Charles Maber (left), with the 6th Earl of Carnarvon in the 1920s.

Above. Groom with one of Lord Porchester's horses and pet dog.

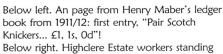

Above. Highclere gardeners with William Pope, (centre with beard and dark hat). The team, led by Mr Pope, "won all the prizes in 2 consecutive years with vegetables grown at Highclere for Lord Carnarvon, at the Shrewsbury Show and thus earned possession on the Cup [inset]. This was later presented back to Shrewsbury Horticultural Society/Flower Show by the family as the William Pope Cup".

Picture and story courtesy of Dr C F Slade, great grandson of William Pope.

Above. The Roll of Honour of Highclere Estate employees who served in the Great War, 1914-1918. There are 75 names on the Roll above, of whom 13 are named as 'Killed', among them G. Digweed of the gardening family. Major J.A. Rutherford is 'Mentioned for Valuable Services'.

Major JA Rutherford, Estate Manager to the 5th Earl of Carnarvon, pictured here front centre, with his 5 sons, all of whom served in the Great War. Three of the sons are listed as 'Invalided'.

Picture and details courtesy of Bertie Rutherford, son of Edward J Y Rutherford (front right), the eldest of the sons.

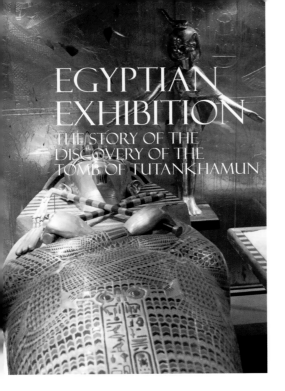

EGYPTIAN EXHIBITION
THE STORY OF THE DISCOVERY OF THE TOMB OF TUTANKHAMUN

The Tomb of Tutankhamun, "The Boy Pharaoh", is one of the most dazzling and wonderful archaeological discoveries ever made. The two names linked inextricably with the historic find are those of Carnarvon and Carter.

The 5th Earl first travelled to Egypt in 1898. His fascination with Egypt followed a series of motor car accidents, as a result of which he was advised to spend winters in a warm climate.

Above. The 5th Earl of Carnarvon. His many motor car accidents forced him to seek warm climes to recuperate. He chose Egypt...

He travelled to the Winter Palace Hotel in Luxor on the banks of the River Nile and developed a compelling fascination with ancient Egypt, its art and its civilisation.

Initially, he worked alone, applying for concessions through the Department of Antiquities, whose director was the eminent French Egyptologist, Gaston Maspero. Increasingly obsessed by ancient Egypt, Carnarvon needed a partner to work with. Maspero introduced him to an out-of-work artist and Egyptologist, Howard Carter. The two men worked together for the next 16 years, becoming firm friends.

Lord Carnarvon paid Carter a handsome salary and built him a house jokingly called "Castle Carter" on the road to the Valley of the Kings. Thereafter, Carter was able to develop some financial stability and to concentrate on their excavation projects. Carnarvon's wealth allowed him to run up to five excavation projects during any one season.

Due to the stifling summer heat, excavation work was carried out for only 3 or 4 months during the winter. The results were then examined and researched before the following season. Carnarvon organised concessions in the Valley of the Nobles and the Valley of the Queens during the following five years.

At the end of this time, he published the results and photographs of their work in "Five Years at Thebes", commissioning the best Egyptology experts to write various chapters of the book. Carnarvon's and Carter's work during this period was notable and would have substantially increased the body of knowledge of ancient Egypt at that time.

During these years, Lord Carnarvon established an impressive collection of Egyptian antiquities, assembling a collection of rare and beautiful works of art but ever spurred on to find something even more beautiful.

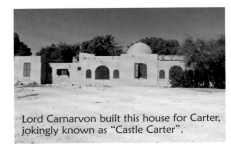

Lord Carnarvon built this house for Carter, jokingly known as "Castle Carter".

Sir Ernest Budge of the British Museum wrote that:

"He only cared for the best and nothing but the best would satisfy him and, having obtained the best, he persisted in believing that there must be somewhere something better than the best. His taste was faultless and his instinct for the true and genuine

Above. Howard Carter who worked with Lord Carnarvon for 16 years.

was un-rivalled." When compared to a beautiful antique, money had no value for him. He used to say that it is easier to get money than antiques.

After 7 to 8 years, Lord Carnarvon was keen to apply for a concession to work in the Valley of the Kings. An American excavator, Theodore Davis, had held the concession for some years but eventually gave it up in 1914, declaring there was nothing more to find.

Above. One of the 5th Earl of Carnarvon's early digs: an 18th Dynasty tomb of Teta-Ky, a King's son who was found to be Mayor of Thebes (modern day Luxor).

The first few years in the Valley were disappointing, yielding almost nothing except for 1920: 6 of a set of 13 alabaster jars were found which had contained oils used in the mummification of Merenptah (1213-1204 BC), ruler of Egypt four generations after Tutankhamun's time.

The Countess of Carnarvon was present on this expedition and was so excited, she dug them up from the mud with her bare hands.

By this time, 1920, Lord Carnarvon was increasingly struggling financially. He could no longer continue to finance excavations in Egypt. The Great War had depleted his Estates and, with increased taxes and the recession beginning to deepen in 1921, he

Above. One of the ancient exhibits in the Exhibition: A rushwork model sieve and collection of wooden and bronze instruments and tools (1390-1353BC), including three small flint blades and two small arrowheads.

told Carter he would have to conclude his efforts in Egypt. However, Howard Carter persuaded him to continue for one more season, the winter expedition of 1922. Carter travelled to Egypt in October 1922, ahead of Lord Carnarvon.

Right. A view of just one of the many colossal 'digs' which Lord Carnarvon financed, this one near Queen Hatshepsut's Temple in the Valley of the Kings.

After some weeks work on a new excavation site in the Valley of the Kings, Carter sent one of the most exciting telegrams ever:

> "At last have made wonderful discovery in valley a magnificent tomb with seals intact; recovered for your arrival. Congratulations Carter."

Lord Carnarvon and his daughter, Lady Evelyn Herbert, travelled to Egypt as swiftly as they could, arriving in Luxor about two weeks later on November 23rd, 1922. They were met with great ceremony by the Governor of Qena Province and Howard Carter.

Over the next two days, rubble was cleared from the sloping passageway of the tomb. Carter was, at last, able to knock a hole through the door.

As the gap was widened they began to see the antechamber packed with chariots, statues, furniture and gold "everywhere the glint of gold".

In the Exhibition in the Castle, this fragment of limestone "stela" dates from the 12th Dynasty, about 4,000 years old. It tells the story of a Chamberlain called Intef.

Further inside the antechamber were three further rooms, including one which was found to contain the golden shrine and coffins of Tutankhamun.

The Pharaoh Tutankhamun (1332-1323 BC) was a minor King, barely mentioned in history, yet this royal tomb dated from one of the most sophisticated periods of Egyptian history.

In the Egyptain Exhibition, a collection of bronze and silver bracelets (c.304-30BC) found by Lord Carnarvon at Tell el-Balamun in the Nile Delta in 1911.

It proved to be packed floor to ceiling with treasures. The discovery of this tomb has bestowed upon the names of Carnarvon and Carter near legendary status, even today.

The find made headlines throughout the world. The Press descended on Carnarvon,

An electrum (an alloy of gold and silver) statuette of a boy named Amenemheb, discovered by Carnarvon and Carter in 1911, in "Tomb 37" underneath the Temple of Queen Hatshepsut in the Valley of the Kings.

Carter and the Valley of the Kings. Hordes of tourists and journalists arrived. Cinemas

played clips throughout the UK and America.

Rumours flared that Tutankhamun's body was being taken back to Highclere. Denials failed to quell rumours and rows flared up between all parties, especially as Carnarvon had given "The Times" newspaper exclusive coverage of the story, to the dismay and fury of the rest of the world's Press.

Carnarvon was, after many weeks of wrangling with the world's media, exhausted and sailed up the River Nile to Aswan for a few days rest. He then returned to Cairo to deal with the authorities and plan the next stage of the process of emptying and conserving the tomb.

He was completely exhausted and had nicked a mosquito bite whilst shaving. The wound had become infected. Septicaemia and fever set in.

His wife, the 5th Countess, flew in a specially chartered biplane from England to be by his side. His son, Lord Porchester, travelled from Mesopotamia (modern day Iraq)

Above. One of the calcite jars found in 1920, showing the cartouche of Ramesses II.

where he was serving with the British Army. Lord Carnarvon died with his family by his bedside on April 5th, 1923, at the Continental Hotel in Cairo.

At the precise moment of his death, the lights went out in Cairo and, eerily, back home at Highclere Castle, his favourite dog Susie suddenly died.

Rumour soon circulated that a legendary curse of the Pharaohs had killed the Earl of Carnarvon.

Left. Howard Carter's map, drawn from 1917 to 1921, of the Valley of the Kings which Carnarvon and Carter used to discover the tomb of Tutankhamun. (By kind permission of the British Museum).

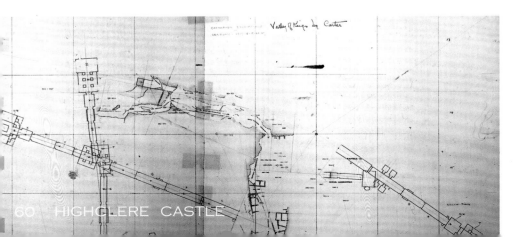

Above. The Grand Opening of the Tomb of Tutankhamun in 1923. Lord Carnarvon is in front with white-banded hat.

Right. On display in the Egyptian Exhibition, a faithful replica of the Death Mask of Tutankhamun.

Below. The 7th Earl of Carnarvon, right, pictured in 1987 with his butler, Robert Taylor, as they discovered the Egyptian artefacts which Howard Carter had described as being "a few uninteresting items", now on display in the Egyptian Exhibition in Highclere Castle.

It had been the ultimate archaeological quest. It nearly had not succeeded. Lord Carnarvon had died at the very hour of his discovery, leaving Carter to work on alone for the following ten years.

After 16 long years of work, they had finally discovered the greatest find in the history of archaeological exploration

Today, almost 100 years later, the 5th Earl's great grandson, the 8th Earl, together with the 8th Countess, have opened an extensive new Exhibition in the cellars of Highclere Castle celebrating his illustrious great grandfather's achievements.

The Exhibition tells the story of the 5th Earl's life from the late Victorian period to the time, just after the end of the Great War, of this great discovery.

Left. Lord Carnarvon's actual razor which he used on that fateful day. On display in the Egyptian Exhibition.

CARNARVON RACING

The various photographs at the Castle of racing colours and trophies celebrate the interest and activities of four generations of the family in bloodstock and racing since the earliest years of the 20th century.

The Highclere Stud was established in 1902 by the 5th Earl of Carnarvon, whose outstanding broodmares, Jongleuse and Malva, produced many winners. Their lines were later re-introduced to Highclere (through Jo-Jo and Minstrel Girl) and the bloodstock further strengthened by the purchase of pedigree colts and fillies from the USA.

In 1905, the 5th Earl became one of the Stewards at the newly established Newbury Racecourse and the family has maintained the connection ever since. His son, the 6th Earl, as well as being a successful breeder of racehorses, was also an amateur jockey in his own right and his exuberant personality made him as well known a figure on the race track, as at the bloodstock sales.

The 7th Earl was Racing Manager to HM the Queen from 1969, until his death in 2001. He was instrumental, while chairman of the Jockey Club Pattern Committee, in setting the Group system as the internationally recognised structure of flat racing today.

Top. "Niche" (Risk Me/Cubby Hole) 1990 ch.f. Shown with proud owner the 7th Earl of Carnarvon.

Right. The 6th Earl of Carnarvon at Highclere Stud in the 1930s.

The present Lord Carnarvon, his brother and sister continue the family's involvement and love of racing today.

Lady Carolyn Warren runs Highclere Stud with her husband and the Hon. Harry Herbert runs the successful Highclere Thoroughbred Racing syndicate business.

Lord Carnarvon races under his own colours and take shares in his brother's syndicates.

Gold, silver and crystal trophies commemorate successes such as the Ascot Gold Cup (Little Wolf 1983), the Yorkshire Oaks Rosebowl (Roseate Tern 1983), the Doncaster Handicap Silver Teapot (Drum Taps 1989) and three Cartier Championship trophies (Lyric Fantasy 1992, Lemon Soufflé 1993 and Tamarisk 1998).

The 6th Earl and Lord Porchester (later the 7th Earl) studying form at the Ritz Hotel, London, c. 1946/47.

100 YEARS OF HIGHCLERE RACING

Facing Page. "Niche" (Risk Me/Cubby Hole) 1990 ch.f. Shown opposite with the 7th Earl. Won 6 races including Falmouth Stakes, Newmarket, Lowther Stakes, York, Nell Gwyn Stakes, Newmarket and Norfolk Stakes at Royal Ascot. Tragically killed in a road accident in 1993.

Top left. Lemon Soufflé (Salse/Melodrama) 1991 b.f. Bred at Highclere, Champion 2 year old filly in Europe in 1993. Joint top-rated 2 year old in Ireland in 1993. Winner of 5 races including Moyglare Stud St. Gr.I., Falmouth St., Cherry.

Left. Lord Porchester (later the 7th Earl) on "Jim Carew" at Kimble Point-to-Point, 1937.

Above right. Lyric Fantasy (Tate Gallery/Flying Melody) 1990 b.f. Winner of 5 races as a 2 year old including The Queen Mary St. Royal Ascot, Sales Supersprint Newbury, The Nunthorpe St. York (Group 1). Last 2 year old to run in the Nunthorpe. She was bought at the Sales as a yearling by Lord Carnarvon.

THE PARK

Left. The approach to Highclere Castle.
Above. The Castle from the south in mid-winter.
Below. The view across the south lawns to the north slopes of Siddown Hill.
Lower left. A view across to the "Wood of Goodwill".
Lower right. The road through Highclere Park.

Highclere Castle is set in 1,000 acres of sweeping parkland. Today, the parkland and gardens provide acres of peace and tranquillity. The walks and views lead visitors through different gardens and woods or along ancient footpaths, with breathtaking views across the rolling downlands of North Hampshire.

The significance of the Park at Highclere is that the landscape still contains features from medieval times and before. There are layers of landscape history showing how our ancestors lived and farmed.

Field systems, lynchets and tumuli lie within the Park and date from the Bronze Age and the Iron Age.

Later, during medieval times, the fields were emparked to create a deer park for the Bishops of Winchester. William of Wykeham then created at least two further deer parks as well as enclosing rabbit and hare warrens. Records from his tenure (1370), show five fish ponds at Milford, on the northern boundary of the estate.

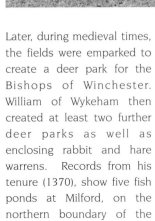

Robert Herbert (1697-1769) inherited the Estate from his grandfather, Sir Robert Sawyer (portrait on page 52, Dining Room).

He embarked on a period of design and enhancement, focusing on using architecture and geometrical design to create views and observation points to "wonder at and admire" the landscape.

The Castle Archives suggest that he designed and built twelve follies in the park surrounding Highclere Placehouse, of which five remain today.

These follies are: "The Temple of Diana", "Heaven's Gate", "Jackdaws Castle", "Etruscan Temple" and "Andover Lodge".

Top left. The Castle from the south.

Top right. A view from the north across the Park to the Castle with "Heaven's Gate" on Siddown Hill on the horizon.

Right. Across the East Lawns to "Jackdaws Castle".

Below. A snow covered Cedar in the Park.

Below left. A distant view of the "Temple of Diana", one of Robert Herbert's 18th century follies.

Andover Lodge

Seen below in an 19th century etching, this folly, sometimes known locally as "Dan's Lodge", was one of the buildings erected by Robert Herbert in the 1740s.

It is situated to the south west of the Estate on the old cross country road towards the nearby town of Andover.

Temple of Diana

This romantic building (above and on the opposite page) sits above Dunsmere Lake. It both provides a point from which to glimpse the Castle and can itself be seen from different observation points in the Park.

The Temple has been restored by the present Lord Carnarvon with the help of English Heritage, Basingstoke District and Hampshire County Council. Visitors are welcome to walk to see it in the summer months.

THE ANDOVER LODGE
Hugh Gore.

Left is a view across the Park on the road to the present day entrance known as "Cherrycot Cottage" Gate.

The side road seen in the picture is the road which takes the visitor to the "Temple of Diana".

This road was the main road into the Park during the 19th century and, after passing by the Temple, continues on to the "London Lodge Gate" which, in those times, was the main entrance to the Park.

Etruscan Temple

This small building, seen above, was probably moved here from its original position in another part of the garden.

It would have sat in an amphitheatre, but now looks towards the wildernesses and Park.

Top left. A modern day view of "The Temple of Diana".
Above. "The Etruscan Temple".
Below. "Heaven's Gate" on Siddown Hill.

Heaven's Gate

Heaven's Gate (pictured right) lies on the summit of Siddown Hill to the south of the Castle.

It was restored and stabilised by the present Earl in 1997, hence the inscription: "*Construit Robert Herbert 1737, restuit George Herbert 1997*".

Whilst it originally had some small rooms and a courtyard, it is now simply a pedimented central arch which frame the views to and from the Castle.

Jackdaws Castle

Above, this was built in 1743 by Robert Herbert to the east of the House and would have been at the far end of the pleasure gardens. It was built using Corinthian columns salvaged from Berkeley House in London, which had burned down in 1733. It acts less as a view point than a temple to be admired from Highclere Castle.

London Lodge Gate

This Gate, above, was once the main Entrance to the Park. In September 1866, Benjamin Disraeli passed through this Gate as he came to stay at the Castle. On passing The Temple of Diana, he exclaimed: "How scenical, how scenical".

Milford Lake

During the first two weekends in May and throughout the summer, visitors are able to enjoy walks around Milford Lake, below, which uniquely retains the rhododendron planting from the 1820s.

The woodland gardens around Milford Lake were much loved and developed by the present Earl's parents with help from Jim Russell.

The walks today reflect a heritage of exotic trees and azaleas, views across a serene lake with many different birds and glimpses into the medieval history of this area as you cross old lynchets.

Left and below. Two views of Milford Lake. Left is the Lake today and below shows a rowing boat on the Lake in a 19th century etching.

THE WINCHESTER LODGE.

Beacon Hill Gate

This Gate, above, was once a main entrance to the Estate. It is also known as "The Winchester Lodge", as it is situated on the main road from the Castle south to Winchester, the county town of Hampshire.

In 1770, Capability Brown was commissioned to draw up proposals for Highclere Park. His proposals are shown on a plan now hanging in Highclere Castle.

The 1st Earl of Carnarvon implemented many of his suggestions, but also complemented them with his own visions.

The drives leading to the Castle were changed, field boundaries swept away, arable land put down to grass, trees and woodlands planted and lakes created.

"Capability" Brown was at the forefront of the new English style of landscape gardening replacing formal gardens with naturalistic compositions. The scale and scope of his work at Highclere show his design in both what he chose to emphasise and what he chose to subordinate.

THE GARDENS

A new bed with many different textures, from euphorbias, to Russian sage, grasses, astrantia, dark lobelia and snapdragons lies in front of the Peach House, which still grows peaches and roses for cutting for the Castle.

Behind a tall yew hedge, lies a white border, created by the 7th Earl and Countess.

The earliest record of a garden at Highclere dates from 1218, which had 61 fruit trees. In 1364, a new garden was created of 44 apple and 27 pear trees, probably within the present walled garden, south east of the House. This is still called the Monks' Garden today.

The walls and arches survive from the Georgian period and the roses, lawns and layout reflects the changed needs of the family.

Today, the walls and arches are still planted with fruit trees: crab apples, quinces and

figs. Lawns, however, have replaced the orchard, yew arches give focal points and roses and lavender surround the lawns.

A gate leads from the white border into the Secret Garden, a curving English herbaceous border originally designed for the 6th Earl of Carnarvon by Jim Russell. Cherry trees and daffodils are scattered through the borders to presage Spring, but the borders come into their own in the Summer months.

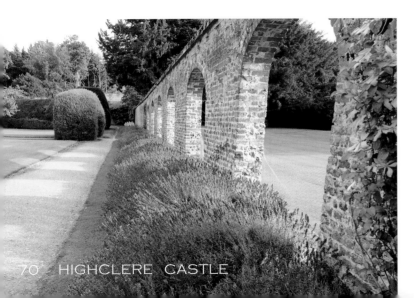

Winding down through the Secret Garden, you can follow the path into the new "wilderness": The Wood of Goodwill.

This area has been restored in recognition of the landscape work of Robert Herbert.

Much of his work and most avenues were swept away by Capability Brown, but the present Earl and Countess of Carnarvon

have re-instated a beech avenue and a central axis in the Wood which now leads to a mount on which used to stand a Rotunda.

Around the Avenue in the wilderness, beech and oak have been re-planted. Some trees are a gift from friends, others planted in memory of longstanding staff at Highclere, both past and present.

From the Wood of Goodwill a path leads through newly planted walnut trees into a Wild Garden. Throughout these woods and wild areas, a collection of tree species native to England has been planted.

A wooden gate at the end of the Wild Garden leads out to a path and short walk, uphill through Penelope's Wood and back to the Castle Lawns.

The South Lawns also overlook a Wild Flower Meadow, a haven for bees and small wildlife.

749	Bishops of Winchester acquire the Highclere Estate.
By 1208	Deer park enclosed and some form of hunting lodge built.
1370s	William of Wykeham starts rebuilding Bishop's Palace at Highclere
1551	Highclere sequestered by Edward VI and sold to William Fitzwilliam.
1572	Highclere purchased by Sir Robert Kingsmill of Sydmonton, whose daughter Constance married Sir Thomas Lucy of Charlecote.
1616	Sir John Lucy builds "Highclere Placehouse very handsome...the front double built with brick and koyned with freestone" and adds a large gatehouse and stables.
1679	Highclere purchased by Sir Robert Sawyer, whose daughter Margaret married Thomas Herbert, 8th Earl of Pembroke.
1692	Margaret Lady Pembroke inherits Highclere. At this date, the house is approached from the south, past an ornamental avenue of beech trees (the Long Walk), and near the new avenue of lime trees.
1706	Lady Pembroke dies, and her second son, Robert Sawyer Herbert, inherits Highclere.
1739	Heaven's Gate built on Siddown Hill.
1743	Jackdaw's Castle "lately erected" beyond the east lawn.
1769	Robert Sawyer Herbert dies and his nephew, Henry Herbert, inherits Highclere.
1770	Capability Brown surveys Highclere, converts Medieval fish ponds into Milford Lake and recommends the creation of Dunsmere.
1774-76	Henry Herbert commissions William Burt to remodel the house as a classical mansion, encasing it in Bath stone and moving its main entrance to the north side.
1793	London Lodge built as the main entrance to the Park, to honour Henry Herbert's creation as the 1st Earl of Carnarvon.
1820s	Thomas Hopper rebuilds the east wing and enlarges the house in "a style Grecian Ionic" for the 2nd Earl.
1838-50	Sir Charles Barry remodels the exterior of the house for the 3rd Earl, encasing it in Bath stone and adding the Great Tower and four corner towers in 1842. Plans to rebuild the parish church abandoned.
1850s	Thomas Allom starts to complete the interiors of the Castle for the 4th Earl, and builds a new west wing as servants' quarters. He also builds the Cemetery Chapel in the Park in 1855.
1870	George Gilbert Scott designs the new parish church, beyond the Park gate by Highclere village.
1890s	Electricity installed in the Castle (1897). Interiors modernised at the 5th Countess's behest.
1914-18	Castle houses a military hospital, run by the 5th Countess.
1939-45	Part of the Castle houses London evacuees; southern part of the Estate requisitioned by the Army.
1988	Gradual refurbishment of Castle is begun by the 7th Earl and Countess, and the Castle is opened to the public.
2003	The Stewardship of the Castle & Estate is inherited by the 8th Earl and Countess of Carnarvon.

The Castle from Heaven's Gate

HIGHCLERE TODAY

Highclere Castle has been the ancestral home of the Earls of Carnarvon for over 300 years. Today, the Castle is still the family home of the 8th Earl and Countess of Carnarvon.

The 8th Countess of Carnarvon, has written a book on her predecessor, Lady Almina, the 5th Countess who converted Highclere Castle into a Hospital in September 1914. The book tells the extraordinary story of life before, during and after the Great War, following Almina's marriage to the 5th Earl of Carnarvon in 1895.

"Lady Almina" has been in the New York Times bestsellers list for 48 weeks.

It is available direct from Highclere Castle or from Amazon or bookshops in the UK and the USA, where it is published by Random House. It has been translated into other languages and sold in many other countries.

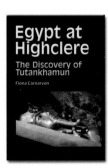

Lady Carnarvon's latest title is "Lady Catherine & The Real Downton Abbey", the story of American-born Catherine, 6th Countess of Carnarvon.

It follows Highclere "upstairs and downstairs", during the 1920's and 1930's and then how the world at Highclere changes in the Second World War.

The 8th Countess has also written the illustrated "Egypt at Highclere", exploring the extraordinary discovery of the tomb of Tutankhamun, as well as the exhibition at the Castle.

"Lady Catherine & The Real Downton Abbey", is available in the UK from 12 September 2013 and in the USA from 29 October 2013.

Future illustrated publications from Highclere Castle:

- A Year at Highclere, the Real Downton Abbey. Anecdotes, stories, extracts from visitor books, interspersed with recipes, gardening tips and stunning photographs.
- Recipes from Highclere Castle. The Real Downton Abbey. Seasonal recipes, cooking for royalty and politicians over centuries, everyday suppers, recipes from fruit trees, vegetables and herbs at Highclere.

Written by Fiona Carnarvon.

With thanks to my husband for editing skills, Duncan MacDougall for book design and typesetting and David Rymill, our Archivist, as well as the guides and all the team who bring the Castle alive for visitors with their warmth, anecdotes and knowledge.

Photography by Elizabeth Vickers and Lord Carnarvon.
Produced by Highclere Enterprises LLP. Printed in the United Kingdom.
For further copies, visit www.highclerecastle.co.uk
© Highclere Enterprises LLP 2013. E&OE. All rights reserved.

Highclere Castle and its Grounds provide a perfect setting for a wide range of public, private, corporate and filming events.

For more information, please telephone the Castle Office on 01635 253210 or email theoffice@highclerecastle.co.uk

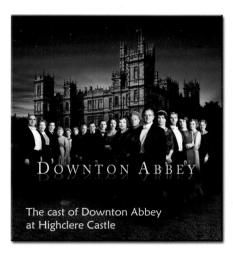

The cast of Downton Abbey at Highclere Castle

Private Tours

Weddings

Corporate Entertaining

HIGHCLERE CASTLE
NEWBURY RG20 9RN

Tel: 01635 253210   Fax: 01635 255315
theoffice@highclerecastle.co.uk   www.highclerecastle.co.uk

Highclere Enterprises LLP   Highclere Castle   Highclere Park   Newbury RG20 9RN
A Limited Liability Partnership registered in England and Wales.   Registered No: OC 305641
Registered Office: The Estate Office   Highclere Park   Newbury RG20 9RN

ISBN 978-0-9926599-1-2

9 780992 659912